C

U

4

2 . JUL 20

WITHDRA

ST SUSSEX COUN

D0410987

Schools Library & Museum Service
Unit D
Ropemaker Park
HAILSHAM
East Sussex BN27 3GU
Tel: 01323 466380

A IS FOR AARDVARK
OF COURSE

SIMON DREW

an alphabet
for the sophisticated youngster
or the puerile adult

SCHOOLS LIBRARY SERVICE

170332-I

Antique Collectors' Club

to Caroline

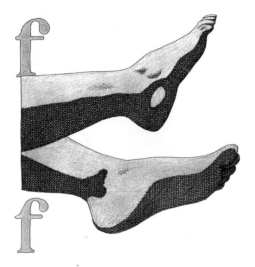

F is for Fry-up with egg
and Flatcap hung up on a peg.
And also for Ferret,
a beast of some merit,
and Foot (at the end of your leg).

East Sussex
Schools Library Service

Supplier: Amazon
Date: 07-04-2015
Invoice: DrSO9k9TK

Mixed Sources
Product group from well-managed
forests, controlled sources and
re-cycled wood or fiber
www.fsc.org Cert no. XXX-XXX-XXX
© 1996 Forest Stewardship Council

©2010 Simon Drew
World copyright reserved

ISBN 978-1-85149-654-9

British Library Cataloguing-in-Publication Data
A catalogue record for this book is available from the British Library

All rights reserved. No part of this publication may be reproduced, stored in a retrieval
system, or transmitted in any form or by any means electronic, mechanical, photocopying,
recording or otherwise, without the prior permission of the publisher

The right of Simon Drew to be identified as author of this work has been asserted by him in
accordance with the Copyright, Designs and Patents Act 1988

Printed in Italy for the Antique Collectors' Club Ltd., Woodbridge, Suffolk

A is for Aardvark of course :
it's a beast that can eat like a horse.
    And Ants start with A . . . .
        and an aardvark would say
that they taste a bit better with sauce.

B is for Boa constrictor
when squeezing it's always the victor.
On the Ark, an old Boa
squashed sweet Mrs. Noah;
by giving a wink, it had tricked her.

B is for Badgers in sets :
they've often been known to take bets
    on the chance that a horse
    cannot finish a course.
(They usually end up with debts).

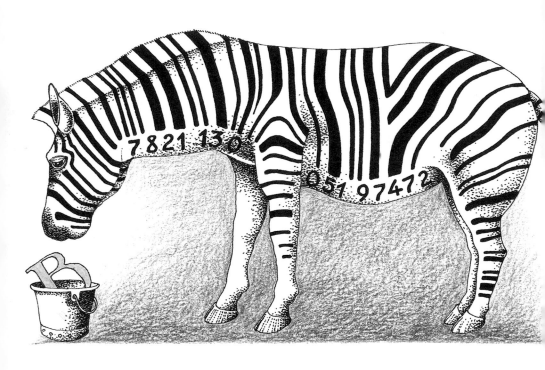

B is a Barcode's first letter.
Try knitting the shape in a sweater;
    then capture a horse -
    fit the sweater by force,
and the zebra you get looks much better.

C is for Cabbage and Collie
and Christmases decked out in holly.
    The Prince of Wales, he
      also starts with a C
though some say he's gone off his trolley.

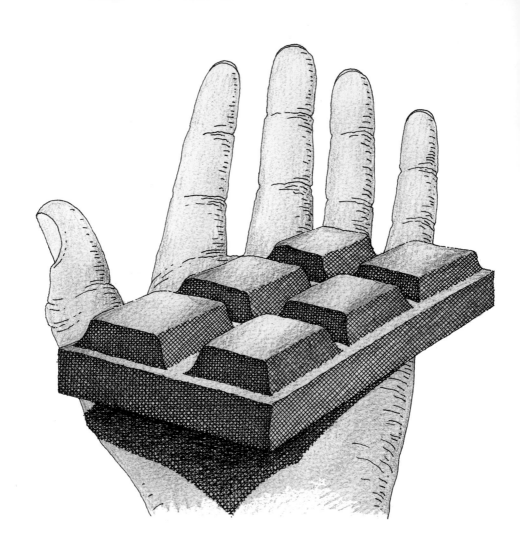

C is for Chocolate and Cake:
to overindulge a mistake.
Try putting a chunk
on the side of your bunk;
to see if your willpower will break.

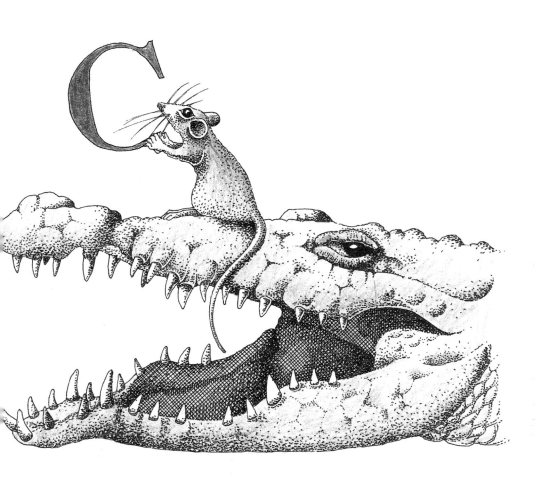

C is for Crocodile-smile:
it's seen on the banks of the Nile.
   A Croc needing tea
     calls a mouse: "Come to me;
why not sit in my mouth for a while."

D is for Dogs that have spots:
Dalmatians are known to have lots.
But sometimes you'll see
a Dalmatian spot-free
but only in shirts and culottes.

D, is for Dog with a tick:
it's nibbling itself till it's sick.
Eventually found,
spits the tick on the ground;
then gives it to me with a lick.

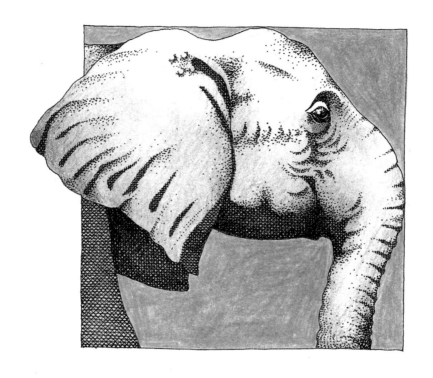

E is for Elephant's Ear.
They say that they use them to hear.
The truth is, I'm told,
when an Elephant's old
the Ear-flapping helps him to steer.

E is for Ego and Eye
though I only starts with an I
    and I'm hoping that E
    will find something for tea
though I think it's just pie in the sky.

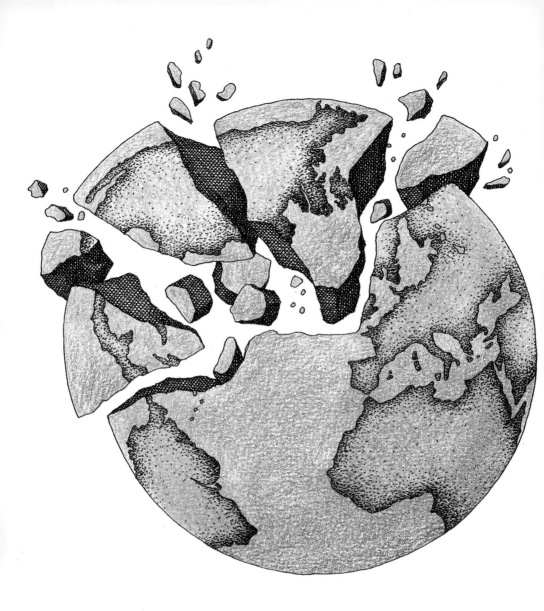

E is for End of the world
when national flags will be furled.
But, no need to fret;
it won't happen yet ...

E is for Earthworm and Eel:
they're slimy and make people squeal.
But which would be crowned
most perfect and round?
It seems only time will reveal.

F is for (nuclear) Fusion.
F is for Fish (try the goujon).
The Future is F
but some men are deaf
for F is for Foregone conclusion.

16

F is for Ferret and Figs
and the Fur that is made into wigs
and F is for Fly
(it is obvious why),
and F is for Frightening pigs.

17

G is the start of Giraffe,
a beast with a very long scarf.
If you hear a low sound
like a noise underground
it's the start of an imminent laugh.

H is for Hare on your Head:
(it doesn't grow on when you're dead).
    Some people say
     it never goes grey:
it's the light shining through it instead.

I is for Igloo and Ice
and Inuit.   Take my advice:
    if you want a good meal
        and you're fed up with seal,
fly south at whatever the price.

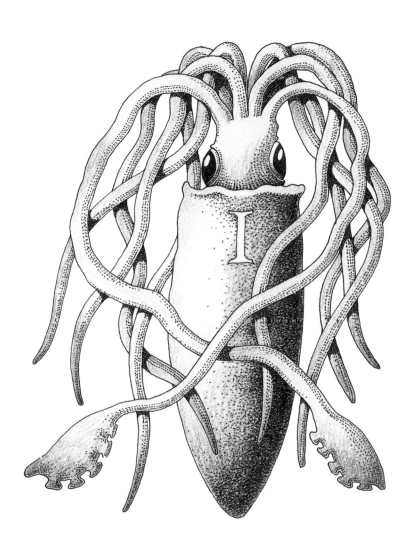

I is the Ink in a squid
which daily writes down what it did.
This animal's eye
is the largest, they cry:
so it must have the biggest Eye-lid.

J is for Jackals that howl,
and more Jungle beasties that prowl
in the dead of night,
but not out of sight
of the Jolly nocturnal wise owl.

K is the Kite on the heath
and Knickers we wear underneath
    between neck and Knee;
        but don't ask to see
for K is for Kick in the teeth.

K is for Kitchen sink dramas:
it's where you would wash your pyjamas.
  And though it's not big
    you might find a pig
in the sink. (It was put there by farmers).

L is the Lion that roars
when you step on its sensitive paws
and L is for Larks
and a Lapdog that barks
and the Lice that the Lapdog ignores.

M is for Money and Mud
and the Masher we use on the spud,
and M is the Mutton
I stole (I'm a glutton),
and M is for Mercy, M'lud.

M is for Moths round a light:
they seem just a blur in the night.
And Mayflies in grief
whose lives are so brief.
And M is Mosquitoes that bite.

N is for Nothing at all:
it's the space you can see on a wall.
  In tennis, as well,
    there's Nothing to tell:
it's the bit you can't see in the ball.

I'm never quite sure about O.
It starts off an Ostrich, although
   an Olive is fine,
   and Orange divine,
an Otter's a rotter, you know.

P is for Peas in a Pod,
Potatoes deep-fried with a cod.
But if you are poor
and you want a bit more
then P is for Prayer sent to god.

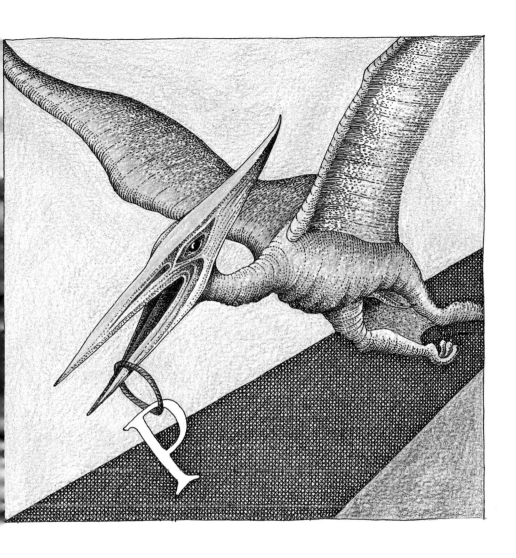

Pterodactyl must start with a P.
The reason is easy to see:
    an absent P error
      would start it with Terror —
this angel could not harm a flea.

Q is the Queen of the land,
the one with an orb in her hand.
You might hear her sigh:
"My husband and I
are thinking of forming a band."

R is for Rhythm in song
or Rattlesnake, deadly and long.
   R is for Rabbits
     with great breeding habits
and R is for Right, never Wrong.

R is for Rubbish and Rot
which is Reeking, recycled or not.
While R is for Riches,
(because of some hitches)
it's Riches we haven't quite got.

Hippopotamus ends with an S :
it's an animal living with mess.
With a bath full of rust
and layers of dust,
housework just causes it Stress.

S is the Slime behind Snails
and the Scum that you clean from your nails
and S is the Slug
that you find in your mug
and S is the Sperm - made in whales.

T is for Turtle-neck sweater:
it's quite like a jumper but wetter.
These Turtles are bred
to hang round your head
so Throats feeling sore will get better.

T is for Tyrannosaurus :
this dinosaur lived long before us.
Books on this theme
are obsessed it would seem;
in fact it's beginning to bore us.

T is the Truffle that grows
in the soil, and is found with the nose
of a sensitive hog
or a highly-trained dog.
It's expensive to buy, I suppose.

U is for Underground mole
who lives half his life in a hole.
But when in your garden,
to make his toes harden,
kicks snails through your veg and shouts 'go

U is for Underground train
where no-one need fret about rain.
You travel together:
you're Under the weather.
Umbrellas not needed again.

V is for Vicar at prayer,
his scalp is revealed through his hair.
He's worn the same vest
since he last had a guest
and the tyre underneath is a spare.

V is for Vegetable stew:
I've a recipe here that is new.
   Even Hannibal Lecter
   would kill for this nectar:
please get to the back of the Q.

W makes us say Why . . . .
is it usually blue in the sky?
And Why's Water Wet
(you don't know, I'll bet)
and Why doesn't Why start with Y?

If there wasn't an X would we care?
It's only crossed sticks in the air.
But Xmas, I fear,
would quite disappear:
no Santa is too much to bear.

Y is for Yellow and Yolk:
and it sounds like a very old joke
but, if Y is for Yak
and it put on a mac,
could it stand in the rain for a smoke?

46

So you finally end up with Z
and Zebras must enter your head:
    they used to wear checks
    and ties round their necks,
but now they're just stripey instead.

What would we do without Z ?
It hovers above us in bed.
The U.S. , you see,
pronounce it as Zee
so what do they think I've just said?